My Grandma Likes to Cook

A mi abuela le gusta cocinar

School Specialty Publishing

Published by School Specialty Publishing, a member of the School Specialty Family.

©℗ 2007 Twin Sisters IP, LLC. All Rights Reserved.

Send inquiries to:
School Specialty Publishing
8720 Orion Place
Columbus, Ohio 43240-2111

Credits:

Executive Producers: Kim Mitzo Thompson, Karen Mitzo Hilderbrand
Illustrated by: Roberta Collier-Morales
Designed by: Steven DeWitt
Published by: Twin Sisters Productions, LLC
Readers: Dixie Higham, Galen Oakes, Austin Thompson,
    Morgan Thompson, Kim Thompson, Hal Wright (English)
    Sal Barbera, Daniela Fernandez, Rafael Mendez
    Carol Trexler, Erick Valle (Spanish)
Translated by: Carol A. Trexler
Music by: Hal Wright
Written by: Kim Mitzo Thompson, Karen Mitzo Hilderbrand

ISBN: 0-7696-4624-7

2 3 4 5 6 7 8 9 10 WAF 10 09 08 07

This is my Grandma.
She is a good cook.

My family likes to
eat dinner together.

"Please pass the chicken and rice," Dad says.

"Please pass the
salad," Mom says.

"I love the applesauce,
Grandma," I say.

"Thank you. Now eat some
corn," Grandma says.

"May I have some bread and butter?" Grandpa asks.

"Yes," Grandma says.
"And here are some beans."

"Please pass me the milk," my brother says.

"Here you go," Mom says.

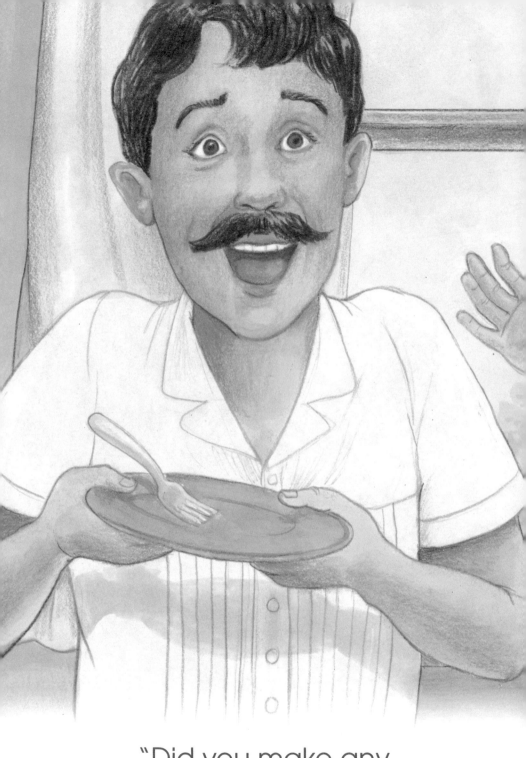

"Did you make any dessert?" Dad asks.

"Did you make any
dessert?" Grandpa asks.

"Of course I made dessert,"
Grandma says.

"I made a great big
chocolate cake!"

chicken and rice
pollo y arroz

salad
ensalada

apple sauce
salsa de manzanas

corn
maíz

pan y mantequilla
bread and butter

beans
frijoles

milk
leche

dessert
postre

chocolate cake
torta de chocolate

thank you
gracias

—¡Hice una gran torta de chocolate! —

—Claro que preparé un postre, — dice mi abuela.

—¿Preparaste un postre? —
pregunta mi abuelo.

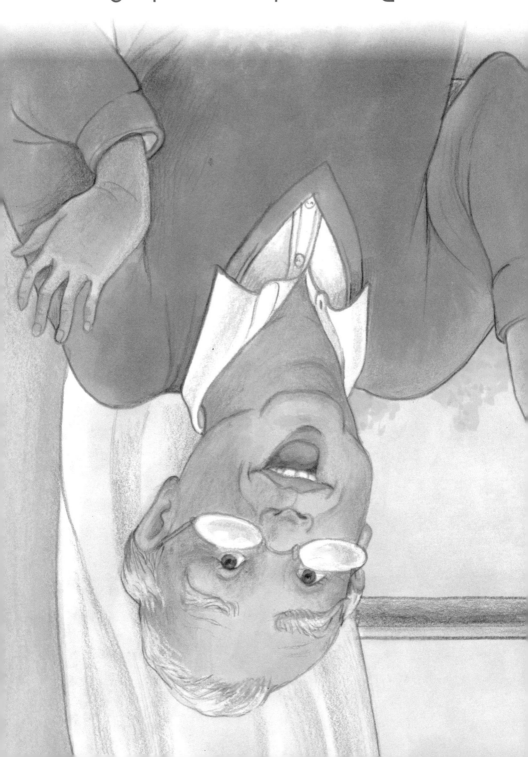

—¿Preparaste un postre? — pregunta mi papá.

—Aquí va —, dice mi mamá.

—Por favor páseme la leche —, dice mi hermano.

—Sí, — dice mi abuela.
—Y aquí hay frijoles —.

—¿Me dan un poco de pan y
mantequilla? — pide mi abuelo.

—Gracias. Ahora come un poco
de maíz —, dice mi abuela.

—Me gusta la salsa de manzanas, abuela —, digo yo.

—Por favor pasa la
ensalada —, dice mi mamá.

—Por favor pasa el pollo
y el arroz —, dice mi papá.

En mi familia nos
gusta cenar juntos.

Esta es mi abuela.
Ella cocina muy bien.

A mi abuela le gusta cocinar

My Grandma Likes to Cook

Publicado por School Specialty Publishing, un miembro de School Specialty Family.

©℗ 2007 Twin Sisters IP, LLC. Todos los derechos reservados.

Envíe sus preguntas a:
School Specialty Publishing
8720 Orion Place
Columbus, OH 43240-2111 USA

Créditos:

Productores ejecutivos: Kim Mitzo Thompson, Karen Mitzo Hilderbrand

Ilustrado por: Roberta Collier-Morales

Diseñado por: Steven DeWitt

Publicado por: Twin Sisters Productions, LLC

Narrado por: Dixie Higham, Galen Oakes, Austin Thompson,
Morgan Thompson, Kim Thompson, Hal Wright (inglés)
Sal Barbera, Daniela Fernandez, Rafael Mendez
Carol Trexler, Erick Valle (español)

Traducido por: Carol A. Trexler

La música por: Hal Wright

Escrito por: Kim Mitzo Thompson, Karen Mitzo Hilderbrand

ISBN: 0-7696-4624-7

2 3 4 5 6 7 8 9 10 WAF 10 09 08 07